UNDERSTANDING COMPUTER SEARCH AND RESEARCH

Paul Mason

heinemann
raintree

© 2015 Heinemann Raintree
an imprint of Capstone Global Library, LLC
Chicago, Illinois

To contact Capstone Global Library, please call 800-747-4992, or visit our web site
www.capstonepub.com

Edited by Linda Staniford and Chris Harbo
Designed by Richard Parker and Tim Bond
Original illustrations © Capstone Global Library 2015
Illustrated by Nigel Dobbyn (Beehive Illustration)
Picture research by Jo Miller
Production by Victoria Fitzgerald
Originated by Capstone Global Library Ltd
Printed and bound in China by CTPS

18 17 16 15 14
10 9 8 7 6 5 4 3 2 1

Library of Congress Cataloging-in-Publication Data
Mason, Paul, 1967-
  Understanding computer search and research / Paul Mason.
      pages cm.—(Understanding computing)
  Includes bibliographical references and index.
  ISBN 978-1-4846-0903-3 (hb)—ISBN 978-1-4846-0908-8 (pb)—ISBN 978-1-4846-0918-7 (ebook) 1.
Internet searching—Juvenile literature. 2. Internet research—Juvenile literature. I. Title.

  ZA4230.M37 2015
  025.0425—dc23   2014015581

This book has been officially leveled by using the F&P Text Level Gradient™ Leveling System.

Acknowledgments
We would like to thank the following for permission to reproduce photographs:

Alamy: Business/Stephen Barnes, 19 bottom right, © ianmurray, 38, SCPhotos, 31 bottom right,
© Sami Sarkis RLD, 13, © wonderlandstock, 7; Getty Images: Hulton Archive / Stringer, 29, Getty
Images Sport/Jeff Kardas, 12, Dorling Kindersley/Steve Lyne, 17; iStockphoto: ©airn, 32 bottom,
© ac_bnphotos, 27 inset, ©bogdansemenescu, 4, ©4kodiak, 27, Shutterstock: Blend Images, 24,
Jaromir Chalabala, 15(dog), gillmar15 (cat), Glovatskiy, 20, Kamira, 40, Viktoria Kazakova, cover,
kellyreekolibry, 31 top left, Dan Kosmayer, 36, mikeledray, 22, Monkey Business Images, 34, 41,
michaeljung, 43, Sergey Novikov, 19 top left, DavidPinoPhotography, 32 top, Schubbel, 15, Jaren Jai
Wicklund, 35.

Design Elements: Shutterstock: HunThomas, vectorlib.com (throughout)
Jaren Jai Wicklund

We would like to thank Andrew Connell for his invaluable help in the preparation of this book.

CONTENTS

Introduction: What's the Difference Between Search
    and Research? 4

Chapter 1: How Does a Computer Search Work?...................8

Chapter 2: What Makes an Effective Search? 16

Chapter 3: How Do You Turn Search into Research? 22

Chapter 4: How Do You Turn Research into Results?............... 32

Conclusion: Top 10 Tips for Search and Research..................42

Glossary..44

Find Out More 46

Index 48

Some words are shown in bold, **like this**. You can find out what they mean by looking in the glossary.

INTRODUCTION: WHAT'S THE DIFFERENCE BETWEEN SEARCH AND RESEARCH?

Using a computer to search and to do research are two different things. Searching is the first step, when you use a computer to find information. Research is the second step—looking at the information carefully, to decide whether it is useful.

Computer trick or treat

One way to understand the difference between searching and researching is to compare it to trick-or-treating. First, you go out and gather as much candy as possible. This is like the "search" phase.

▲Before getting a puppy, you need to find out how to care for it. The Internet would be one good place to search.

Once the candy-gathering phase is finished, you can examine the loot. In one pile, you put the things you want to keep. In another pile are the items that you don't want. This is like the research phase—deciding which information to keep, and which to abandon.

THE KNOWLEDGE

The first-ever tool for searching the Internet was invented in 1990. It was called Archie—*archive* without the *v*. The first true search engine was probably W3Catalog, which appeared in 1993.

Searching and the Internet

It is possible to search for information on your own computer's **hard drive**—for example, by looking at an encyclopedia that has been stored there. However, almost all computer searching and researching is done on the Internet, using a **search engine**.

Fox Terriers - Image Results

More **Fox Terriers** images

Fox Terrier - Wikipedia, the free encyclopedia
en.wikipedia.org/wiki/Fox_terrier   Cached
History | Modern breeds | Common health issues | References
Fox Terriers are two different breeds of the **terrier** dog type: the Smooth **Fox Terrier** and the Wire **Fox Terrier**. Both of these breeds originated in the 19th century ...

Smooth **Fox Terrier** Information and Pictures, Smooth **Fox** ...
www.dogbreedinfo.com/smoothfoxterrier.htm   Cached
All about the Smooth **Fox Terrier**, info, pictures, rescues, care, temperament, health, puppies and much more

◀This shows the first three web pages from a total of over two million found by an Internet search engine. They *all* contain information about fox terrier puppies. Deciding which ones are the most useful will require some research.

TECHNICALLY SPEAKING

For understanding the Internet and how it works, the technical knowledge in these boxes will be useful. For example, you might want to know how to keep **spiders** out of your computer—but these are not creepy crawlies! Turn to page 10 to find out the truth.

What is the Internet?

The Internet is a network of computers that covers most of the world. It is made up of lots of different kinds of computers, plus the connections between them. Many computers connect to the Internet using the phone system.

The network allows computers to send information back and forth. It is like a huge, incredibly high-speed postal service. But it sends **virtual** communications from one computer to another, rather than sending actual letters and packages.

True and false on the Internet

The Internet is not like school, where a teacher gives you a lower grade if what you have written is not correct. On the Internet, there are no grades that tell you whether something you read is true or false. Even web sites that look professional may contain false information. Only research can tell computer users whether the information they find on the Internet is correct.

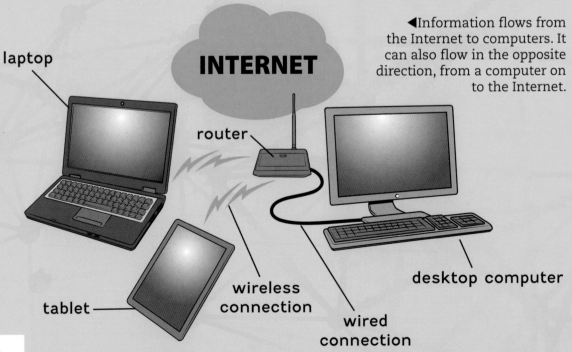

◀Information flows from the Internet to computers. It can also flow in the opposite direction, from a computer on to the Internet.

laptop

INTERNET

router

wireless connection

tablet

wired connection

desktop computer

▲The Internet has lots of sources of information, including many different kinds of text, videos, photos, and artwork.

THE KNOWLEDGE

Almost any computer can be used for searching and researching. It is usually easiest on a computer with a fairly big screen, since this makes information easier to read. Best are probably:

- desktop computers
- laptop computers
- tablets and mini tablets/notebooks.

Internet searches can also be done on e-readers, smartphones, and some video game consoles.

TECHNICALLY SPEAKING

The Internet is a global network of computers. The web (sometimes called the World Wide Web) is made up of information contained on the Internet.

7

CHAPTER 1: HOW DOES A COMPUTER SEARCH WORK?

Computers search the Internet by using a search engine. There are lots of different search engines. There are important differences between them (see pages 18 and 19 to find out more), but most work in a similar basic way.

Collecting information

Search engines find and organize information from the Internet. First, they go through the Internet, looking on web sites for particular words. For example, the search engine might look on web sites for "puppies" or "basketball."

Next, the search engine makes a list, or **index**, of the sites that use the words it has searched for. Under "puppies," it would list sites that mentioned that word. A site that uses the word a lot gets a higher place in the index than one that only uses it a few times.

Search Engine Market Share, February 2012

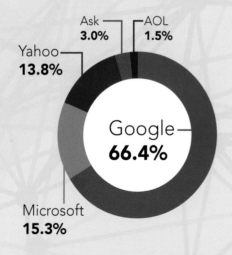

Ask **3.0%**
AOL **1.5%**
Yahoo **13.8%**
Google **66.4%**
Microsoft **15.3%**

▲In 2012, Google was the most-used search engine by far. A good researcher uses a variety of search engines, not only one.

THE KNOWLEDGE

Today's most popular search engines have indexed hundreds of millions of Internet entries. They handle tens of millions of searches every 24 hours. Search engines never sleep. They add hundreds of web pages to their indexes every second.

Pointing searchers to the right place

When someone begins a computer search, the search engine checks its index. Where on the Internet can the searcher find information about puppies, for example? The engine lists the pages it has found that mention them, in page after page of results.

One important thing to remember about search engines is that they do not search the whole Internet every time you do a search. They search their own index of the Internet.

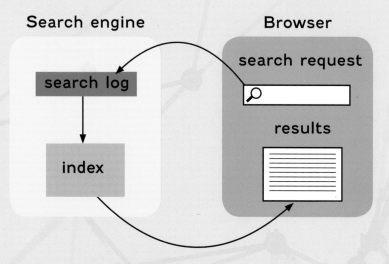

Try this!

Ask an adult to help you do two Internet searches for "fox terrier puppy care." Use Google for one search and DuckDuckGo for the other. The results will be different. This tells you that the two search engines have different indexes.

Spider indexes

Search engines build up their indexes using spiders! These spiders don't have long legs or scare people who are frightened of our eight-legged friends. They are actually **software robots**. They crawl around on the web, looking for whatever the search engine has told them to look for.

The spider begins its journey at a popular web site or **server**. It records the words it finds there (although usually it skips common words such as *the* and *a*). The spider also often notices where on the page words are found. Words in a heading, for example, are more likely to be important.

Having indexed one site, the spider then follows any **links** to other sites. The spider indexes these new sites, then follows *their* links to still more sites. A group of spiders can index hundreds of web pages per second, so they can quickly build up an enormous index.

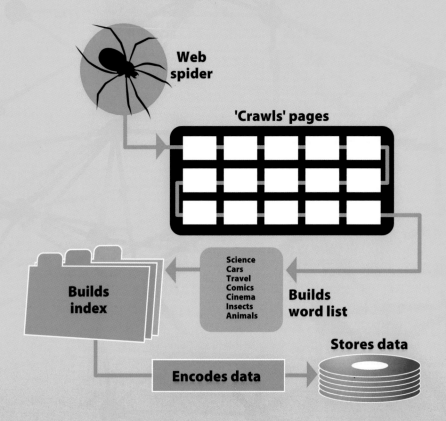

Web spider

'Crawls' pages

Science
Cars
Travel
Comics
Cinema
Insects
Animals

Builds index

Builds word list

Stores data

Encodes data

THE KNOWLEDGE

Web site designers often add links (the full name for these is "**hyperlinks**") to the site. These are words or images that, when you click on them, take you to other web sites or other parts of the site you are on. The link leads you to more information, an explanation, or a new subject that is connected to the one you are reading about.

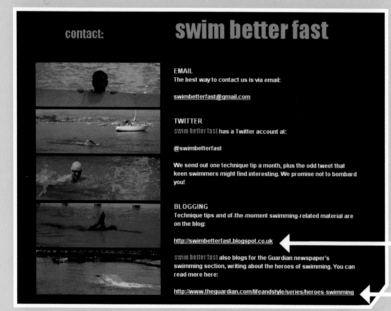

hyperlink

hyperlink

TECHNICALLY SPEAKING

Not all search engines take the
same approach to indexing:

• At one extreme, they may index every word.
• At the other extreme, a search engine may
index only headings, subheadings, **meta tags** (see
page 12), and the most frequently used words.

Most search engines fall somewhere
between the two extremes.

▲This shows supercross star Bubba Stewart. He has lots of fans—but what are the best places to find Bubba on the Internet? Hopefully, meta tags will help!

Meta tags

Meta tags are a way to make spiders take special notice of something on a web page. The person who creates the web page sets up the tags. They are like hanging up a sign for the spiders, saying, "Get your information here!"

The owner of a fan site for the American supercross star Bubba Stewart, for example, might add meta tags for "Bubba Stewart," "supercross," "SX," "fan," "African American," and "racer." When an indexing spider crawls through the site, it will know these words were especially important. People doing a search for "African American supercross racer" will be more likely to be directed to the site.

Tricky taggers!

Some web site owners try to attract visitors to their site by adding meta tags for popular subjects (for example, "World Series tickets," "One Direction," or "Leonardo di Caprio"). The trouble is, the sites do not actually have any information about these subjects! Thankfully, indexing spiders are too smart to be fooled. They compare the meta tags with the words that actually appear on the site. If the two don't agree, the spiders ignore the meta tag.

TECHNICALLY SPEAKING

There are a *lot* of indexing spiders crawling around the Internet. Some sites—for example, gaming sites—change all the time. Having spiders crawling through them recording changes would slow the game play down. So, the site owners set a robot exclusion protocol, which stops the spiders from crawling through their web pages.

▲Without the robot exclusion protocol, the Internet games played on computers would probably work noticeably more slowly.

Boolean operators

Boolean operators are words such as *and, or, not, followed by,* and *near.* They are part of the language of Internet searches. Using these words is a good way to get exactly the search results you want. The most common are shown on these pages:

and

Putting *and* between words means that only pages that contain all the words will appear in search results. (The search engine will not look for *and,* just the other words.) Some search engines use + instead of *and.*

or

Putting *or* between two (or more) words will mean that at least one of the words must be featured on a web site for it to be included in the search results.

not

This is a way of making sure things do not appear in your search results. You might, for instance, search for "Boston and City not Red Sox," to prevent Boston Red Sox sites from appearing.

followed by

Only web sites where the words appear in exactly the order you have given will be listed. For example, "Yellowstone followed by horseback riding" would produce only web sites that feature results relating to horseback riding in Yellowstone National Park.

near

This is short for *within 10 words.* So, searching for "California near surfing" will produce a list of web sites where the words *California* and *surfing* appear no more than 10 words from one another.

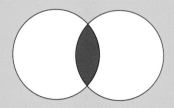

AND

= only material featuring a dog AND a cat

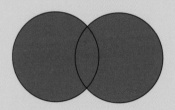

OR

= material featuring a dog OR a cat

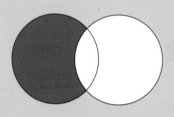

NOT

= featuring a dog, but NOT a cat

▲Using the right Boolean operators will help you get the exact results you want.

Try this!

To see how Boolean operators can affect a search, try this:

1. Search for "fox and terrier and puppy and care."

2. Open a new window, but use the same search engine to search for "fox terrier puppy care."

3. Compare the two windows. The results will be different—the Boolean operators have affected them.

CHAPTER 2: WHAT MAKES AN EFFECTIVE SEARCH?

Computers cannot read anyone's mind. They can only do what people ask them to do. So, putting a vague subject into a search engine will produce vague results. Using carefully chosen search terms will produce more useful results.

General search terms

General search terms can be useful at the beginning of a search. The results provide background information, plus ideas for new search terms.

At this stage, it is important not to let search terms be affected by what you already know. For example, imagine someone writing a report on famous basketball players. A LeBron James fan might be tempted to search for "LeBron James." But a search for "top ten basketball players" would give much wider results.

THE KNOWLEDGE

The following are signs that a web site is likely to contain reliable information:

- Sites with addresses ending in .org, .edu, and .gov, which are often run by government or educational organizations.
- A well-written, clear site with no grammatical or spelling mistakes.
- Clear author qualifications (this includes whether the site is from a credible organization, such as a famous museum).
- Detailed information, with facts rather than opinions.
- Sites that are not trying to sell something (a product or an idea).

TECHNICALLY SPEAKING

Specific search terms

After a general search, the search terms can be made more specific. The basketball report writer, for example, might have found three or four people who appear in every top ten list. Searching for each one by name will give more detailed information about them.

1) You just got a fox terrier puppy, and you need to find information about him on the Internet:

fox terrier puppy

2) The first thing you want to know is whether the puppy needs grooming:

fox terrier + grooming

3) There are two types of fox terriers, with different types of hair!

wire haired fox terrier + grooming

4) You discover your puppy needs a special comb, called a puppy comb, until he is older:

wire haired fox terrier + puppy comb

17

Using a variety of search engines

To get the widest range of search results, experienced researchers use more than one search engine. They do this because not all search engines are the same. For example:

- Some search engines specialize in particular types of information. Someone who wants to find out a computer-game tip, for example, might get good results from a search engine that specializes in the subject.

- Other search engines index only particular areas of the Internet, or unusual types of pages, such as the text from entire books or quotations.

- There are even search engines that collect the results from other search engines.

Specialized engines often produce different results from a general search engine.

Try this!

Use your favorite search engine to look up "tsunami." Now open two new windows and use the same search term in mahalo.com and yippy.com. The results will be different. Which do you think would be the most useful for writing a report?

▲Which place are you most likely to be able to find specialized information? Somewhere that specializes, of course!

THE KNOWLEDGE

There are thousands of search engines on the Internet. These are just a few that work in different ways:

- ask.com: This is a natural-language search engine, which lets you ask a question as if you were asking a teacher or friend.

- yippy.com: This is a "Deep Web" search engine, which indexes pages most indexing spiders do not reach.

- mahalo.com: One of several human-powered engines, Mahalo's index is reviewed by humans before **content** is included.

- duckduckgo.com: This engine suggests ways to narrow down information (called disambiguation).

▲Organizing the results of your computer research makes it much easier to find the information you need at any given moment. Otherwise, each time you want to remind yourself of something, you will probably end up looking through your entire set of results.

THE KNOWLEDGE

One way to save results from an Internet search is to cut and paste interesting information into a new document. The trouble with cut and paste, though, is that it is easy to forget where the information came from. Some people even get confused and think someone else's work is their own. To avoid this, always make a note of where information has come from.

Organizing results

Good researchers organize their search results. It makes it easier to find specific pieces of information later. There are several ways to do this:

1. Print out

The printouts can be organized into folders (or just piles). A good way to start is with file names using your original specific search terms. For the project on pages 16 and 17, there could be a folder called "top tens" and other folders for each famous basketball player.

2. Save on the computer

It's also possible to save search results onto the computer. Like the piles of paper, the results can be organized using folders and **subfolders** on your computer's hard drive.

3. Save web addresses

Search results can be saved in the form of web addresses, which you can go back to later. It is important to take notes about what information the web site holds. For example, an article on tsunamis might have web sites listed under headings such as "recent examples," "history," and "causes." Each web site listed would also need a short description, such as, "2004 tsunami Indian Ocean."

p.16
[A]
WHAT MAKES AN EFFECTIVE SEARCH?
https://blogs.glowscotland.org.uk/fa/ICTFalkirkPrimaries/tag/google/
http://primarytech.global2.vic.edu.au/2012/05/29/tentips-for-teaching-students-how-to-research-and-filter-information/

[intro]
Computers cannot read anyone's mind. They can only do what people ask them to do. So, putting a vague subject into a search engine will produce vague results. Using carefully chosen search terms will produce more-useful results.
37

[B]
1) General search terms
General search terms can be useful at the beginning of a search. The results provide background information, plus ideas for new search terms.

At this stage, it is important not to let search terms be affected by what you already know. For example, imagine someone writing a report on famous England footballers. A David Beckham fan might be tempted to search for "David Beckham". But a search for "top ten English footballers" would give much wider results.
78

[B]
2) Specific search terms
After a general search, the search terms can be made more specific. The football report writer, for example, might have found three or four people who appear in every top ten list. Searching for each one by name will give more detailed information about them.
45

▲Unless you take notes about where information has come from, and organize your work carefully, you could end up accidentally using someone else's work as your own. This is called plagiarism (see page 36) and is not allowed.

CHAPTER 3: HOW DO YOU TURN SEARCH INTO RESEARCH?

A researcher is like a trick-or-treater who's collected a big bag of candy. The bag might contain some pieces of black licorice that you dislike—yuck! These need to be identified and dumped, so that only the best candy remains.

Sorting information

Information you have searched for and gathered from the Internet is like a trick-or-treater's candy—a mixed bag. Some will probably be incorrect. This incorrect information is the black licorice. It needs to be identified and dumped.

▲A good researcher acts like a detective at a crime scene. Detectives start by finding out everything about the crime. Then they examine the evidence, to decide which pieces are important and which can be ignored.

TECHNICALLY SPEAKING

Crowdsourcing is a name for getting information about a subject from lots of different people. They can all review and change the piece of work (for example, an article about tsunamis). Online sites such as Wikipedia use crowdsourcing to produce their content.

You have to be careful during this process, though—it is easy to feel that something that does not agree with what you already think must be unreliable or inaccurate. This is not necessarily so. When evaluating information, researchers are careful not to let what they think they know affect their results. Instead, they check facts that seem incorrect or surprising, to see whether they are true or not.

THE KNOWLEDGE

Researchers always notice the date when something was written. Dates can be important. For example, if you are looking up the world record for the highest BMX jump, an article from 2005 might not be accurate. The record could easily have been broken since then.

▶When doing research using a computer, remember that not everything you read will be 100 percent reliable. Lots of people who put material on the Internet like to make their opinions sound like facts!

Types of information

There are all kinds of web sites on the Internet. When researching something, it is important to be able to tell one from another. Key types of web sites that appear in search results include:

Content/information sites

Web sites such as Wikipedia, About.com, and the web sites of museums and government departments.

Good things: They often give a clear summary of the subject.

Possible problems: Crowdsourced sites are unlikely to be 100 percent correct, because mistakes are only corrected if someone notices them.

Blogs and microblogs

Blogs and **microblogs** such as Blogger, Wordpress, and Tumblr.

Good things: These are a good way to look at lots of different opinions quickly.

Possible problems: Bloggers sometimes make their opinion look like fact, which can lead to confusion. It is unlikely anyone has checked to see if the writer's work is correct.

Community sites/chatrooms/forums

These are usually about specific interests (for example, BMX racing, surfing, or being in a choir).

Good things: These can be a good **source** of expert advice, with a wide range of opinions.

Possible problems: It is hard to be sure whether the people giving advice are qualified, and some writers think their own opinions are facts.

Question-and-answer sites

Sites where people can send in questions to see if anyone reading knows the answer.

Good things: These are a good way to get a variety of answers quickly.

Possible problems: These sites often give you a "best answer," but it is impossible to know whether the answer is actually correct.

DARRYL! DINNERTIME!

IN A MINUTE. THIS IS IMPORTANT!

WHAT IS?

SOMEONE ON THE INTERNET IS *WRONG!*

◄Correcting every error on the Internet would take a very, very long time.

The CARS checklist

The CARS checklist is a good way to figure out whether a web site is likely to be a good source of useful information. *CARS* stands for "Credibility, Accuracy, Reasonableness, and Support."

CARS 1: Credibility

Credibility is another word for believability. When researchers look at information, they ask themselves: Should we believe this?

For a web site to be believable, the author (who can be an individual writer or an organization) should have experience or education relevant to the subject. Anyone can write an article about tsunami risks, for example. But someone who works for the emergency services, or a government agency, is more likely to know about the subject.

THE KNOWLEDGE

These warning signs suggest that a text is not credible:

1. It is not clear who the author is.
2. There is bad grammar and/or a lot of spelling mistakes.
3. Lots of negative comments appear in the Comments section.
4. The author uses emotional language—for example, "The evil victors murdered thousands of their prisoners in cold blood."

C.A.R.S. ➡ CREDIBILITY
Is the source of the information qualified? ➡

CARS 2: Accuracy

Accuracy simply means correctness. First, find out when something was written, and whether this could have an effect on its accuracy. Even something from a credible source written years ago may not still be accurate today.

Accuracy can also be affected by who an article is aimed at. An article about how engines work that a nine-year-old could understand would not have enough information for an automotive engineer.

▲The Pacific Tree Octopus appears on a very convincing web site—even though there is no such thing as a Pacific Tree Octopus!

THE KNOWLEDGE

These warning signs suggest that a text may be inaccurate:

- There is no date, so it is not clear when the text was written.

- An old date is attached to a text about something new or constantly changing.

- There are lots of general statements that cannot always be true—for example, "The Chicago Bears are boring to watch."

ACCURACY
Is the information recent?
Is it detailed enough?

REASONABLENESS
Is the text balanced and fair?

SUPPORT
Are the facts backed up?

CARS 3: Reasonableness

What makes a source of information reasonable? These three things are important:

1. Reasonable texts admit that there may be more than one view. For example:

   World War I was caused by German aggression.

   vs.

   Many people think German aggression caused World War I. Others say that the actions of Russia and France were also responsible.

   Which seems more reasonable?

2. Reasonable texts do not **contradict** themselves within the same article. For example:

   No one famous has ever come from Maine.

   Then, later in the same article:

   The best-selling author Stephen King was born in Portland, Maine.

   If a best-selling author came from Maine, then he is at least one famous person to have come from that state.

3. If the author's opinion becomes clear to the reader, the text may not be reasonable. The author is probably making a one-sided argument, rather than giving the facts.

   For example:

   Despite the claims, great white sharks have never been proven to attack humans. As I have repeatedly said, the true culprit is always the bull shark.

C.A.R.S. → **CREDIBILITY** Is the source of the information qualified? →

THE KNOWLEDGE

These warning signs suggest that a text is not reasonable:

1. The language is emotional or made personal— for example: "The whole DVD is garbage" or "Anyone who disagrees with this is a fool."
2. There are no facts to support what the text says, or opinions have been put forward as facts.
3. The writer gives a one-sided view, without admitting that other views are possible.

THE KNOWLEDGE

Lots of web sites claim that the nursery rhyme *Sing a Song of Sixpence* was invented as a secret recruiting rhyme for pirate ships. These web sites did not research the story! It is actually a spoof, made up by an **urban-myth** investigation team.

ACCURACY
Is the information recent?
Is it detailed enough?

REASONABLENESS
Is the text balanced and fair?

SUPPORT
Are the facts backed up?

CARS 4: Support

Most information that is available on the Internet comes from somewhere else. For example, an article about how to survive a tsunami is not likely to have been written by someone who has survived a tsunami. Instead, the author will probably have gathered information from several different sources.

A good researcher likes to know what sources an author has used, so that he or she can judge whether they are reliable or not. For example:

Climbing a tree is a stupid thing to do during a tsunami.

vs.

The Pacific Tsunami Center says that climbing a tree is unlikely to save you during a tsunami.

Finally, if an article makes a surprising claim, the author should provide extra support for it. For example:

Cows are bad for the environment.

vs.

Cow burps are causing global warming. The United Nations says that methane—which cows burp out constantly—is one of the most harmful greenhouse gases for the environment.

THE KNOWLEDGE

These warning signs suggest that a text is not well supported:

1. Statistics are given, but without any information about where they came from or when they were produced.
2. The researcher cannot find other sources of information with the same facts. (And even if they can, care is needed—some web sites simply cut and paste text from elsewhere. Check that the exact same words have not been used in two sources.)

▲People who can show where their information came from are always easier to believe than those who cannot.

"No—we need to go up a hill!"

"The government says up a HILL is safer!"

31

CHAPTER 4: HOW DO YOU TURN RESEARCH INTO RESULTS?

Once you have researched a subject, you will have a lot of good-quality information. You will probably be eager to start writing! This chapter shows some of the things good writers do to turn their research into results.

Reorganizing research results

Imagine someone trying to write a 750-word report for people going on vacation in a tsunami zone. Research has given the person a good idea of what information is available. Armed with this, the writer can start sketching out a basic plan for the report. He or she might decide to have five 150-word sections called:

1. What is a tsunami?

2. Are all tsunamis dangerous?

3. What are the warnings a tsunami is coming?

4. Can you prepare for a tsunami?

5. How do you survive a tsunami?

These headings can be used to organize the research. For example, "What is a tsunami?" would have the information on what causes tsunamis, how often they happen, and how big they are. When the writer comes to write that section, all the research will be gathered together ready.

Which is easier to use—organized or disorganized information?

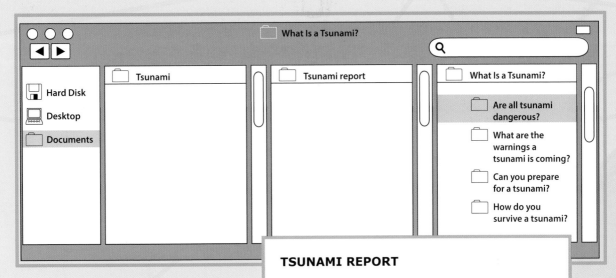

▲Organizing your information into folders and subfolders, like these, is a good way to start turning your research into results.

TSUNAMI REPORT

What is a tsunami?
From the U.S. National Oceanic and Atmospheric Administration:
oceanservice.noaa.gov/facts/tsunami.html

Are all tsunamis dangerous?
News reports on 2013 tsunami
www.usatoday.com/story/news/world/2013/02/07/solomon-islands-tsunami/1897891
www.cnn.com/2013/02/05/world/asia/solomon-islands-quake

Scientific summary of 2004 tsunami:
news.nationalgeographic.com/news/2004/12/1227_041226_tsunami.html

▶Alternatively, you could organize your results in a single document, like this.

THE KNOWLEDGE

Research throws out lots of different types of information, including photos, diagrams, and quotes. There are two ways to organize these:

1. All together in one subfolder—this is best if there are only a few.
2. Separately, with the relevant sections (for example, "What is a tsunami?"). This is best if there are a lot.

▲If you want to publish work on a blog, ask an adult to help you set it up.

Starting to write

To start writing a section—for example, "What is a tsunami?"—the writer opens that folder. Inside will be all the research results for this section. Rereading these before writing reminds the writer of anything he or she has forgotten.

Subsections

Before writing each section, it can be helpful to divide it into subsections. "What is a tsunami?" for example, could be divided into "Causes," "Frequency," and "Size." If the whole section is to be 150 words long, each subsection will need to be about 50 words long.

Where to begin?

Most writers prefer to begin by writing the first section, then the second, and so on. However, as long as the research has been divided into sections, it should be possible to write them in any order.

▲Adding images to a piece of work often makes it more interesting to read, and easier to remember as well.

THE KNOWLEDGE

Photos and artwork can add a lot to a piece of written work. For example, saying that some tsunamis are as tall as a three-story house becomes more real next to a photo of someone standing next to a three-story house! To work well, images should appear close to the words they illustrate.

Respecting other people's work

When turning research into results, it is important to respect other people's work. For example, writers must never pretend that other people's work is their own, or use someone else's work without permission.

Watch out for plagiarism!

Plagiarism is copying someone else's work and pretending it is your own. Writers are allowed to include other people's words and ideas in their work, but they must say where these words and ideas came from. This is called citing or acknowledgment.

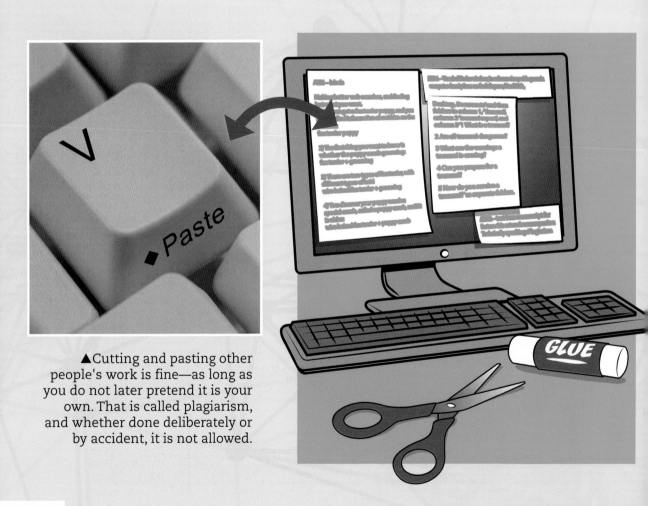

▲Cutting and pasting other people's work is fine—as long as you do not later pretend it is your own. That is called plagiarism, and whether done deliberately or by accident, it is not allowed.

TECHNICALLY SPEAKING
Checking for plagiarism is very easy:

1) There are several plagiarism checkers on the Internet.

2) A quick check is to put suspicious sentences into a search engine, with quotation marks around them. If it has been copied from a web site, the results will show where the sentence appears on the Internet.

Here are two examples. The first is plagiarism, the second is not:

The Zephyr skate team was all conquering. They were unconventional and they didn't care if they got high scores.

vs.

The Zephyr skate team was all conquering. As skating world champion Tom Sims said, "They were unconventional and they didn't care if they got high scores."

Plagiarism is not always this obvious, however. The box below lists some of the other forms of plagiarism.

THE KNOWLEDGE

This is a selection of plagiarism offenses:

1. Copying someone else's work word-for-word.
2. Including big blocks of text that are someone else's words.
3. Using someone else's work but changing a few words so it is not exactly the same.
4. Using someone else's ideas, but slightly rewritten.
5. Mixing proper acknowledgment with unacknowledged use of someone else's work.

▲Although a photo search on the Internet will call up lots of photographs, none of them is yours. It is important not to act as if they are.

Acknowledgment/citing

If a writer uses someone else's work, adding an acknowledgment means no one can accuse him or her of plagiarism. The acknowledgment should say:

- the author's name

- where the original can be found (for example, an Internet address or a book title)

- the date it was written.

If someone wants to know more about a particular subject, they can go to the source to find it. And if the source turns out to be wrong, people will be able to see it was not 100 percent the writer's fault!

Intellectual property

Intellectual property is a way of saying that someone who makes a piece of work owns it. This is common sense—but it can be easy to forget on the Internet. Intellectual property includes writing, photos, videos, and music. On the Internet, these are usually free. Just because it is free for everyone to look at, though, does not mean it actually belongs to everyone.

It is easy to drag and drop photos, artwork, and other content into a piece of work. It is important not to do this unless you are sure that the owner has given permission.

▲Always respect the copyright symbol—even when it is not actually there!

TECHNICALLY SPEAKING

If something has a copyright symbol (©) next to it, it's a reminder that the person who made the work owns it. Even without the copyright symbol, the makers are still the owners unless they say otherwise.

There's a simple rule for whether or not to use someone else's work—"If in doubt, leave it out."

Fact checking and review

Following the right search and research procedures should mean that the facts in a well-researched piece of work are correct. However, everyone makes mistakes! It is easy to write something down incorrectly or get a number wrong, for example. Good writers always check their own work at least twice:

1. The first check is to make sure the finished piece makes sense and that you have not left out anything you wanted to say. If you are checking a piece of work for school, look back at the original assignment. Have you done what was asked?

2. The second check is to make sure all the facts are correct. Check every fact, paying special attention to any that seem suspicious.

It is also useful for someone else to look at a piece of work before it is finished. They sometimes spot mistakes the author has missed.

▲ In addition to checking your own work, it is a great idea to have someone else look at it. He or she can tell you if it makes sense and whether anything could be added or removed.

TECHNICALLY SPEAKING

A peer is a person with similar experience. So, peer review is asking someone like you—someone from school, or the same age—to check your work. Peer reviewers have to be careful not to let their feelings affect their review. Whether the reviewer likes someone or not, he or she should give an honest opinion of the work—not the person!

▲ Having someone like you check through your work once it is finished is called peer review.

THE KNOWLEDGE

Put the fact you want to check into a search engine, and make sure that a reliable source (see pages 26–29) confirms the fact is correct. It is important not to just check the same source again—check that the fact is backed up by a different source.

CONCLUSION: TOP 10 TIPS FOR SEARCH AND RESEARCH

The Internet contains millions of web pages, which contain all kinds of information. Finding exactly what you want can be like looking for a needle in a haystack. Following our Top Ten Tips will make the job easier and give better results.

1. Remember that there is a difference between searching and researching. For good results, you need to do both!

SEARCHING

2. When searching for information, use a variety of search engines. They all have different indexes that will produce different results.

3. Use Boolean operators (see pages 14 and 15) to narrow down your search results.

4. Always note where information comes from, so that you can go back and find it again later. (This also prevents you from forgetting that it is someone else's work.)

RESEARCHING

5. Never think that because something is on a web site, or high up in a search results list, it must be correct.

6. Remember there are all kinds of information on the Internet. Lots of what you read is opinion, not fact.

7. Use the CARS checklist to decide whether a web site is reliable or not.

USING YOUR RESULTS

8. Use the knowledge you have gained through research to make a plan for your work. Use this plan to organize your results.

9. When writing up your results, be careful not to claim other people's work as your own.

10. Always check your work, especially your facts.

◄ Who knows? Maybe if you use a computer really well for researching your schoolwork, it could lead to some prize-winning results.

Try this!

Compare how you would research a subject on the Internet now with how you would have done it before reading this book. Make a list of the new things you would do.

GLOSSARY

blog web site where a writers can publish their work, usually for free. The things they write appear in time order, with the newest first.

blogging writing a blog

content words, images, and design that appear on a web site

contradict disagree with

hard drive disc inside a computer where information is stored. Many desktop computers have hard drives. Laptops, tablets, and phones often use a different kind of storage, called a "solid state drive," or SSD.

hyperlink word or image that, when you click on it, takes you to a web site

index list of items. A search engine's index lists all the information it has found on the Internet.

intellectual property ownership of a piece of work. For example, an article about surviving a tsunami is the intellectual property of the person who wrote it.

link another word for hyperlink

meta tag device making search-engine spiders take special notice of something on a web site

microblog blog that limits people to a small number of words or a very simple layout. The most popular microblogging sites are Twitter and Tumblr.

search engine computer program that people use to find information on the Internet

SEO short for "Search Engine Optimization," a way of making a web site appear higher up in a search engine's results list than it normally would

server super computer designed for a specific task—for example, storing information or running a network

software robot piece of computer code that follows instructions given to it by a human programmer

source where information originally came from

spider on the Internet, a spider is a software robot that works for a search engine, gathering information for the engine's index

subfolder folder contained within another folder

urban myth story that is often repeated, but that no one knows is really true or not

virtual created using a computer

FIND OUT MORE

Books

Cindrich, Sharon. *A Smart Girl's Guide to the Internet* (Be Your Best). Middleton, Wis.: American Girl, 2009.

Hile, Lori. *Social Networks and Blogs* (Mastering Media). Chicago: Raintree, 2011.

Hunter, Nick. *Internet Safety* (Hot Topics). Chicago: Heinemann Library, 2012.

Mason, Paul. *Understanding Computer Safety* (Understanding Computing). Chicago: Heinemann Library, 2015.

Raum, Elizabeth. *The History of the Computer* (Inventions That Changed the World). Chicago: Heinemann Library, 2008.

Internet resources

www.kidrex.org
This search engine works from an index of pages that have been created especially for kids. It relies on the Google search engine's SafeSearchTM filters to screen out unsuitable material.

www.kidsclick.org
This site was designed especially for young people by librarians. You can search by subject, media (photos, sound, and video), or even using the Dewey Decimal System that is found in libraries.

http://kidshealth.org/kid/feeling/school/plagiarism.html#
www.plagiarism.org/plagiarism-101/prevention

Each of these web sites describes plagiarism and gives useful tips on how to avoid committing it.

www.searchenginewatch.com
This is a good place to start finding out about different search engines. Within the site—at http://tinyurl.com/q5r3fkc—is a page giving information about some of the search engines you can use to find just the right search engine! This web site is designed for use by adults, so you'll need to ask an adult to help you use it.

Places to visit

Computer History Museum, Mountain View, California
www.computerhistory.org

Learn about the history of computers at the Computer History Museum. This museum has many fascinating exhibits.

Living Computer Museum, Seattle, Washington
www.livingcomputermuseum.org

The Living Computer Museum was created by Paul G. Allen, the cofounder of Microsoft. The museum explores and preserves the milestones that have led to computer technology today and features many interactive exhibits.

INDEX

accuracy 27, 28
acknowledgment/citing 36, 38–39
"and" (Boolean operator) 14, 15
Archie 4
author qualifications 16

blogs and microblogs 24, 26, 34
Boolean operators 14–15, 42

CARS checklist 26–30, 42
chatrooms 25
community sites 25
computer research 4, 6, 7, 22–41, 42
computer search 4, 5, 6, 7, 8–21, 42
content/information sites 24
contradictions 28
copyright symbol 39
credibility 26, 28
crowdsourcing 23, 24
cut and paste 20, 30, 36

dates 23, 27
desktop computers 7
disambiguation 19

e-readers 7
emotional language 26, 29
errors 24, 25, 26
evaluating information 23

fact checking 23, 40, 41
false information 6
folders and subfolders 21, 33, 34
"followed by" (Boolean operator) 14
forums 25

gaming sites 13
Google 8, 9
grammatical mistakes 16, 26

hard drive 5
human-powered search engines 19

indexes 8, 9, 10, 11, 18, 19
intellectual property 39
Internet 6, 7

laptop computers 7
links 11

meta tags 11, 12–13

"near" (Boolean operator) 14
network 6, 7
"not" (Boolean operator) 14, 15
notebooks 7

one-sided arguments 28, 29
"or" (Boolean operator) 14, 15

peer review 41
photos and artwork 35, 38, 39
plagiarism 21, 36–37, 38
printouts 21

question-and-answer sites 25

reasonableness 28, 29
reliable sources 16, 24–25, 26–29
respecting other people's work 36

reviewing your work 40–41
robot exclusion protocol 13

screen grabs 21
search engines 4, 5, 8–9, 10, 11, 14, 17, 18, 19, 41, 42
search results, organizing 20, 21, 42
search results, saving 20, 21
search terms 16–17
SEO (Search Engine Optimization) 17
servers 10
smartphones 7
software robots 10
spelling mistakes 16, 26
spiders 10, 12, 13, 19
statistics 30
subsections 34
support for information 30–31

tablets and mini tablets 7

urban myths 29

video game consoles 7
virtual communications 6

W3Catalog 4
web site addresses 16, 21
web sites 6, 8, 10, 11, 13, 14, 16, 17, 24–25
what computer research is 4
what computer search is 4
Wikipedia 23, 24
World Wide Web 7
writing out research 32–40, 43